SOCIAL FORTUNE

OR
SOCIAL FATE

A SOCIAL THINKING® GRAPHIC NOVEL MAP FOR SOCIAL QUEST SEEKERS

WATCH THEIR DESTINIES UNFOLD BASED ON THE CHOICES THEY MAKE

Social Thinking®.com

Social Thinking Publishing, San Jose, California
www.socialthinking.com

"With *Social Fortune or Social Fate*, Pamela Crooke and Michelle Garcia Winner promote the idea of social competence (not just social skills) in a way that incorporates research in the areas of visual learning and cognitive behavioral interventions. In addition, their use of the graphic novel as a platform to translate social concepts into complex behavioral repertoires takes a popular medium and uses it in a, potentially, very productive way."

Dr. Peter Gerhardt
Director, McCarton Upper School
New York, New York

"Love the emotion meters, thought and speech bubbles and graphics as a way to help students incorporate and internalize what they have learned from social-behavior mapping and hidden curriculum lessons. This is a great way for teens to learn about their own and others' Social Thinking."

Lydia Garcia Liu, M.S.
Speech Language Pathologist
Tucson, Arizona

"Cool! - The illustrations would appeal to ages 12-17. The facial expressions show what they are feeling. When you flip the book it's like a replay on a social situation."

Tyler Bozetski
High school sophomore, age 16

"Once again Garcia Winner and Crooke have zeroed in on a critical social thinking concept that many of our kids struggle with: making choices and predicting the corresponding consequences. Through clever organization, the authors present 10 social scenarios in anime-style cartoon strips where the characters make their choices and, on the opposite page, discuss the consequences of that choice. Each social scenario begins with a good choice (Fortune) or unexpected choice (Fate). The outcome hinges on perspective taking before making a choice. *Social Fortune or Social Fate* is a must have in the Social Thinking toolbox. Our kids are really enjoying discussing the scenarios and relating them to their own life choices."

David Myford, MSW, LSW
School Social Worker
Communication Development Program
Southwest Cook County Cooperative for Special Education

SOCIAL FORTUNE

OR
SOCIAL FATE

A SOCIAL THINKING® GRAPHIC NOVEL MAP
FOR SOCIAL QUEST SEEKERS

WATCH THEIR DESTINIES UNFOLD BASED ON THE CHOICES THEY MAKE

Pamela Crooke and

Michelle Garcia Winner

Social Thinking.com Jr.

Social Thinking Publishing, San Jose, California
www.socialthinking.com

Social Fortune or Social Fate
A Social Thinking® Graphic Novel Map for Social Quest Seekers

Pamela Crooke and Michelle Garcia Winner

Illustrated by www.tiger-arts.com

Graphic Design by Elizabeth A Blacker, elizabethblacker@me.com

Copyright © 2011 Think Social Publishing, Inc.

Library of Congress Control Number: 2010935012

ISBN: 978-0-9825231-5-5

Social Thinking Publishing
3031 Tisch Way, Suite 800
San Jose, CA 95128
Phone: (877) 464-9278
Fax: (408) 557-8594

This book is printed and bound in Tennessee by Mighty Color Printing.
Books may be ordered online at www.socialthinking.com.

To learn more about Social Thinking® concepts for adolescents, please explore:

Thinking About You Thinking About Me, 2nd edition

Social Behavior Mapping

Socially Curious and Curiously Social (a book for teens to read)

Worksheets! For Teaching Social Thinking and Related Social Skills

....and many more titles.

www.socialthinking.com

SOCIAL FORTUNE TABLE OF CONTENTS

SOCIAL FORTUNE OR SOCIAL FATE

Don't Skip Over This Part....

We know you're tempted to flip to the graphic pages in this book, but we'd like you to know about a few hidden things before you start. You have some choices about how you read this book, and we want to give you all the options first. This book has graphics, maps, hidden letters, emotion meters, and a couple of other things for you to discover. So, hang in there and read the following pages—it will make your quest a better one.

You should know right up front that this graphic novel is all about CHOICES. Have you ever thought about how many choices we all make in a day? It's about a zillion! You know, little things like how long do I brush my teeth this morning, or should I try to find the match to this sock, or where should I put my game control so that my little brother won't touch it? And choices aren't only at home and not just with things. We make choices all day long about what to say (or not to say) to people, whether or not to get into a group, when to ramp up (get super angry), and when to cool down (get relaxed and calm).

Some choices don't seem to matter much, like matching a sock. But other choices are pretty important, especially ones in social situations. That's what this book is about—social choices in social situations and why they matter. But first we've gotta give you the scoop on what we mean by social situations.

You Can't Avoid Them...They're Everywhere

Have you ever noticed that every place you are during the day has a different set of things that you're expected to do and even words you're expected to say? And, what's expected is based on where you are at that moment and the people who are around you. Each time you're supposed to use a different set of social behaviors based on what's happening around you, that's called a social situation. Here are some examples to make this a little clearer. These are just examples, so what's expected of you in your situation will probably be a little different.

Social Situation #1 = Having dinner with the family at home

Place: Home
Time: Evening
Who's there: Maybe some or all family members
What's expected: Depends on the family. Every family has a set of "rules" that are expected during mealtimes. Some might be that you sit at the table, eat your meal with a fork and spoon, clean up after yourself, and on and on. There's a range of what's expected because every family is different.

Social Situation #2 = Eating lunch at school

Place: School
Time: Middle of the day
Who's there: Kids at school
What's expected: Hang out, eat lunch using hands or fork depending on what's for lunch, walk around, read, and on and on. It depends on the school and your age, but every school has a set of "rules" that kids are supposed to figure out for lunch break.

Social Situation #3 = Asking a question in class

Place: School

Time: Most of the time when in class

Who's there: Kids at school and teachers too

What's expected: Depends on the class, but many teachers want you to raise your hand and wait for them to call on you before you ask your question.

IMPORTANT: Every one of us has to figure out or calculate what the RULES are in every social situation!

Rules Are Sometimes Hidden!

In every social situation, there are things that people do and say that are OK (expected) and NOT OK (unexpected) for that exact time and in that particular place. In fact, every time any of us walks into a new social situation, one of the first things we do is try to figure out the rules of that particular situation. We all have to do this! Every single one of us! Sometimes the rules are super easy and clear, and sometimes they are "unspoken" or "hidden." Here are a couple of examples:

Social Situation = Passing other kids in the halls at school

Obvious rules: People are expected to walk (not crawl or slither or roll down the hall).
People carry their own stuff (rather than grab others' backpacks or things).
And on and on…

Hidden rules: It's also expected that kids will accidentally bump into one another in a crowded space. Kids may do things in the halls that aren't OK in class (talk in a loud voice volume, run, etc) but are OK here.
And on and on…

Each social situation has a set of obvious rules and hidden rules, and it sometimes takes a little practice to figure them out. Once you've figured out the hidden rules or what's expected and unexpected in that situation, it's time to make choices.

The cool thing about this is that once we've figured out the rules, we get to make choices about what we say and do or what NOT to say and do. The trick is to know what's expected and then make the choice to do just that! Next, we'll look at some types of ways that people make choices in social situations. Take a minute to think about the choice-maker that best describes YOU. Keep in mind that every choice someone makes around others affects how those people feel about the behavior they observe.

1. Auto-Pilot Reactor:

This person forgets to think about the social situation and so puts his brain on auto-pilot. He doesn't really think too much about the choices he makes and reacts really quickly or without considering how his actions or words might affect others. This person often ends up really confused or angry because his quick reactions cause others to be hurt or angry or annoyed. You'll see some examples of this in the book.

2. Option Resister:

Well, sometimes a person actually does take the time to think about the situation but thinks her way is the only way. This is the kind of choice-making where the person takes a minute to figure out the social situation but forgets to (or doesn't) consider that her choices affect others. In other words, she just thinks about what she thinks is best or easiest or more comfortable for her. There are many examples of this in the book as well.

3. Coin Flipper:

So let's say a person doesn't want to think and instead really wants to rely on chance or the flip of a coin to help him make social choices. There are a couple of problems with this option. First of all, it would be kinda awkward with a coin…walking around the halls and at home flipping and flipping and then making choices based on that. Another problem is that it would only give a person a 50% or so success rate. Not the best idea. There are no Coin Flippers in this book and we hope to never see one.

4. Social Thinker:

This person uses his brain to THINK and then figure out the social situation and use a strategy code (we'll talk about these later) to know what to say or do. This graphic novel has plenty of examples of this type of thinking. You'll see the characters use Social Thinking to figure out what to do in the social situation.

In this book, three characters (Kiko, Rin, and JT) find themselves in a whole bunch of social situations where they have to make choices about what to do and say (or not say). When they do what's expected, their journey follows a map that takes them on the road of SOCIAL FORTUNE. If they do what's unexpected for the situation, the map leads them down the road of SOCIAL FATE. So now we need to explain what we mean by the roads and this special type of map.

Maps and Roads

You know about typical maps, but the map in this book is different. You'll see that the three characters find themselves using this map during every situation. We call it a Social Behavior Map. You'll learn more about it in the next few paragraphs, but the easiest way is to think of it as a map that has two parts. As we said before, if a person makes choices that are expected for that social situation, he is sent down the road to Social Fortune. If she makes choices that are unexpected for the social situation, she ends up on the road to Social Fate. Here's the cool thing. You'll get to see each of the characters make choices that lead him or her down both roads—Social Fortune and Social Fate! You'll see how things can really change for the characters based on what they choose.

Here's how the map works. It all starts with a social situation. Remember, a social situation is just about anytime we're around others and there are rules about what to say or do.

Social Behavior Map

This map is a little different because it goes in a straight line. It starts in the left box and moves to each of the boxes to the right. How a person uses this map determines whether he (or she) goes on a road of Social Fortune or on a road of Social Fate. Take a look at the FIRST box in the road below.

1. What you do affects how another person feels

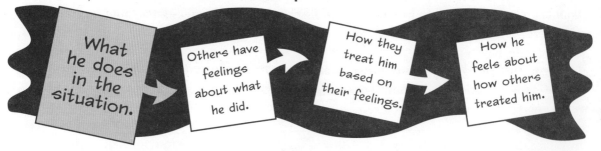

So you can see that the first step on the road is WHAT HE DOES in a social situation. This is where the characters in this book (or you) make a CHOICE about what social action they will take. It could be the movement they do with their bodies, their facial expression, or the words they say or don't say. You can see by the road below that the first box leads directly to the fact that others will have thoughts and feelings about what the person did or said (from the first box). There's an example of what we mean coming up next.

2. Others have feelings about what you do

Here's an example:

Social Situation = Bedtime and mom tells Kiko to turn off the TV

What he did = Said "Yeah, OK mom." And then turned off the TV.

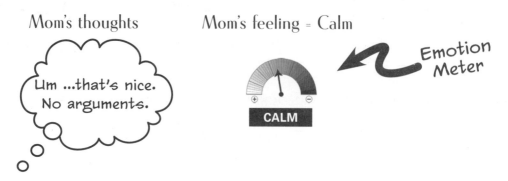

Mom's thoughts

Um ...that's nice. No arguments.

Mom's feeling = Calm

Emotion Meter

CALM

Well it's pretty obvious that Kiko's mom would have some sort of thought about how Kiko reacted to her request. In this case, his mom had a good or positive thought about what Kiko said and did. It's the same for the rest of us. When we do or say something in a social situation, people have thoughts about it AND those thoughts are connected to a feeling! That's why you see the Emotion Meter right next to the mom's thoughts.

3. How people feel about your behavior affects how they treat you

Ok, you get the idea, right? But now let's keep going down the map a little further. The thoughts and feelings of others around us pretty much control how they treat us in that social situation. Take a look at the third box below.

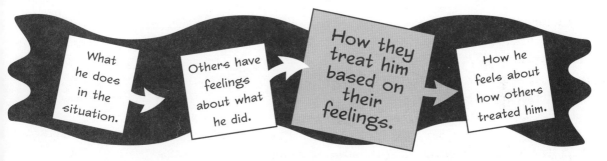

So Mom is feeling calm (which is always a good thing). And because she's calm, she'll react in a way that is calm too. For example, she might say something like, "Thanks for listening," or she might walk away and not nag Kiko to get going. "Avoiding the nag" is a huge accomplishment on his part!!

4. How people treat you affects how you feel about yourself

Finally, the last piece of the map is how Kiko feels about how the other person treated him. This is where you'll see more emotion meters in the book.

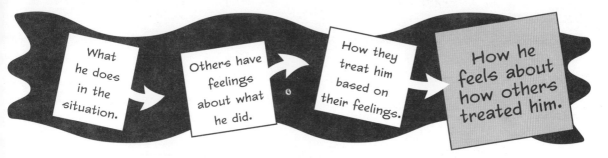

In this case, he can't help but feel "calm" or "relaxed" or even "happy" about the way his mom treated him.

Social Situation = Bedtime and mom tells Kiko to turn off the TV

What he did = Said "Yeah, OK mom." And then turned off the TV.

Mom's thoughts   Mom's feeling = Calm

Um ...that's nice.
No arguments.

CALM

How mom treated him: No nagging today!

How Kiko felt about avoiding the nag:

RELAXED

EMOTION METERS

PROUD

OKAY

FURIOUS

You'll see these meters all through the book. They're really important because the choices that Rin, Kiko, and JT make always leave others around them with a feeling or emotion. When the arrow faces to the left, it means that the person feels "good" or "fantastic" or "proud" or another positive emotion. When the arrow is in the middle, like in the example above, the person feels "neutral" or "calm" or "OK." When the arrow points more to the right, where the meter gets darker, the person feels a more negative emotion like "angry" or "annoyed" or "furious." It's the same for all of us and for you—whenever we say or do something in a social situation, we leave others with a thought and an emotion. That's why the second box on the map shows that others have thoughts and feelings connected to what he or she did.

Realize how fast this all happens!

You can see by the map that it all starts with the choice that our characters make in the social situation. Now, here's something important for real life: it only takes about one or two seconds to move along this map!

Expected and Unexpected behaviors: 2 sides to social behavior mapping

So that's the main idea about the map. But like any map, there's more than one route to take. This map has two roads. The first is the road of SOCIAL FORTUNE. That's the road Kiko took above. It most often has a pretty good ending for our characters because what happens along the way ends up with the person feeling pretty good about themselves. The road of SOCIAL FORTUNE is sometimes called the *Expected* road because the characters figure out what to do in that social situation and do what's expected in that time and place to keep others feeling OK or good or even great!

The other road, or the road of SOCIAL FATE, is often called the *Unexpected* road because the characters make a choice about what to do in that social situation that ends up being not so great because people get upset and treat them in a way they don't like.

Here's an example of the two roads side by side:

Social Situation: Bedtime and mom asks him to turn off the TV

Road of Social FORTUNE

(Expected Road)

Road of Social FATE

(Unexpected Road)

Says "Okay"

Says "NO" or just ignores her

1. What he does in this specific situation

CALM

ANGRY or ANNOYED

2. Others' thoughts and feelings about what he did

Mom says "Thanks" and he avoids the Nag

Mom yells or nags or takes away TV time

3. How they treated him based on those feelings

RELAXED or GOOD

ANGRY or FRUSTRATED

4. How he feels about how she treated him

So here's your first choice!

You can read this comic in a few different ways. If you read the Fortune side first and then the Fate side second, you'll see how all three characters are Social Thinkers and are able to take the road to SOCIAL FORTUNE. If you flip the book over and read the Fate side, you'll see what we mean by the power of "choice." This is where characters make different choices and end up on the road to SOCIAL

FATE. You'll see "Auto-Pilot Reactors" and "Option Resisters" on almost every page. But, you also have a third way to read the book. You can read the graphic story and then flip it over and read what happens when the character makes a different choice. The social situation is exactly the same (top four pictures) on the road to SOCIAL FORTUNE or SOCIAL FATE. What sends the character down one road or the other is the choice the character makes in the picture after the top four where it says "what he/she does." It's amazing to think that one little choice makes such a BIG difference in what happens in the end—but it does! So, it doesn't really matter which way you decide to read this book. It's up to you. Oh, by the way, your parents and teachers may learn a thing or two from this book, but you'll have to teach them how to use it. Most don't know a whole lot about graphic novel type books—they likely won't have a clue.

3 REALLY IMPORTANT THINGS YOU NEED TO KNOW!

1 THINKING ABOUT WHAT PEOPLE THINK ABOUT YOU

So the thing is – we think about each other even when we are not talking. We think about each other when we are just sitting in the same class or passing each other in the hall. People remember when others make them feel comfortable and they remember when people make them feel uncomfortable. In fact, people are more likely to remember when people make them feel upset or uncomfortable. Think about your own social memory. You probably can remember pretty clearly when someone did something to you that made you feel upset. When we are comfortable with a person, we are most likely having normal or good thoughts about that person. When a person makes us feel upset or stressed, we are most likely having uncomfortable or weird thoughts about that person. Here's the deal. The thoughts we have about a person have a direct connection to how we treat him or her. Most of us treat people ok/well when we have good thoughts about them and we are more likely to treat others badly when we have uncomfortable thoughts about them! The same goes for other people; they are likely to treat you the best when they have good thoughts about you and more likely to treat you the worst when they have weird or uncomfortable thoughts about you.

When someone does a "behavior" that causes an uncomfortable or weird thought, people usually call it a "problem behavior." So let's talk about problems!

2 THE SIZE OF THE PROBLEM

Some problems just happen and others are caused by people doing things that make others uncomfortable. But just because we call it a "problem" does not mean we should think of it as a catastrophe! Problems come in different sizes and not all problems require us to solve them with the same urgency or importance. Some problems really are quite small (like size 1,2, or 3) and are sometimes called "glitches." A glitch might be something like breaking your pencil lead or bumping a person by accident. Moderate to medium size problems (size 4, 5, 6 or 7) could be something like losing your cell phone or calling someone a jerk! A big problem (size 8, 9 or 10) is one that upsets a lot of people and usually causes physical or money problems. This kind of problem is like when someone in your family gets in a car accident or a parent loses his or her job or there's a big natural disaster (like an earthquake or hurricane that comes close to you)! It is important to figure out how big a problem really is, because if you over-react to any size of problem, others can feel awkward, uncomfortable, or just plain annoyed. A big reaction to a problem means you're blasting your emotions in a really huge way. So the question is...How much emotion should you let fly out when you're really upset and how much is supposed to stay in? That's the next thing we need to talk about!

3 EMOTION EXPRESSION COMPRESSION

You already know that four-year-olds can go from super upset to goofy-happy. But something happens when we all get older – we are supposed to get better at controlling how we express our emotions especially when out in public, like at school. Social rules and expectations change with age and we all have to figure that out. This doesn't mean we don't have emotions! We can still get upset or really happy when we are at school, it is just expected that we down-play our feelings so that people perceive us to be relatively calm even when we are upset! We call this Emotion Expression Compression, or in everyday words – *Feel it Big on the Inside but Express it Smaller when in Public* (FBI-ESP). By the time we are in upper elementary school or beyond, others are more comfortable when feelings come out in "little bursts" rather than a blast of emotion. So, here's an example: If Kyle is really, really mad – others around him feel okay if he shows that he's a little irritated. But, if Kyle blows his emotions like a volcano, then others around him are uncomfortable with the lava flow of anger and now he's created another problem with them. Or, if Chandra thinks something is hilarious in class, her best bet (or best choice in this case) is to just smile or laugh a little rather than launch into a crazy laughing fit.

FBI-ESP: (**F**eel it **B**ig on the **I**nside but **E**xpress it **S**maller when in **P**ublic.) One strategy people use when they are feeling really big emotions on the inside and know they need to keep the size of their expression smaller on the outside is to take a couple of deep breathes when feeling really upset and then think about the fact that others will have really uncomfortable thoughts if they emit a burst of emotion in public.

We teach little kids that the size of the problem is supposed to match pretty closely to the emotions others see coming from them. So, if someone is having a size 5 problem, then it is OK for that little kid to show a size 5 reaction, which means they are acting pretty upset. But, like we said earlier, kids in upper elementary school and all the way into adulthood are supposed to play down their reactions to problems. So if they have a size 5 problem, they are supposed to stay pretty calm (like a size 1,2,3 response) while trying to repair their problem. An example of repairing would be that the kid explains the problem while keeping his voice and face mostly calm.

WARNING: Big negative reactions (looking/acting really upset) will make your teachers and other kids upset too and then you've got a whole new set of problems because everyone is feeling their own emotions because of your big reaction. An example might be if Antonio has a big 'ol temper tantrum in the classroom. The teacher might feel frazzled, concerned, angry, disappointed, distracted or just plain annoyed. The other students may feel frustrated, threatened, embarrassed or irritated at Antonio. Ugh. This cycle of emotions just isn't good for anyone around Antonio. So you see…these emotions are really powerful and that's why we're giving you a big "heads-up" (meaning pay attention) so you'll know what to do the next time you get into a situation where a reaction might happen.

IMPORTANT: We know that sometimes things happen and you just need a good cry or yell. We also understand that you might need to talk with someone to help you figure out the size of your problem or why your emotions feel so huge. So, if it feels like your emotional volcano is always ready to blow no matter where you are, then you should ask someone in your family or a teacher/counselor at school to help. All of us, including adults, still have to think about FBI-ESP and they might have some strategies to help you.

CHECK OUT THE PROBLEM SOLVING THERMOMETER AND FBI-ESP STRATEGY in the middle of this book. It's a reminder that your reaction needs to be smaller than the size of the problem itself!

Social Behavior Maps, Quest Tips, and Strategy Codes

After you read the graphic story on the left side of the page, you'll see a map on the right side. Remember, the beginning of the book showed a visual map that had four squares. This is exactly that same map, but we've filled it in for you. You'll see the social situation at the top of the page and then four columns. These columns are the same as the four map squares. These boxes have a Quest Tip and Strategy Codes. The Quest Tips talk a little about what happened in the social situation. Twelve different Strategy Codes show what each of the characters did during the journey to SOCIAL FORTUNE. You probably already noticed the strategy codes that are listed on the insides of both covers. If you didn't, you can take a look at them now or just wait to see them while you are reading the graphic stories.

Hidden Letters

Each page that has a comic story has a hidden letter somewhere in the graphics. Once you find all 20, you'll be able to put them together to decode the Words of Wisdom in the spaces below. To see an example, go to the graphic story on page Fortune/2. The hidden letter "Y" on this one is pretty obvious because it's on the boy's shirt in the third picture. The rest of the hidden letters won't be quite so easy. In fact, some are kinda tricky.

Start at the beginning of the SOCIAL FORTUNE side of the book. When you find each letter, write it on a sheet of paper or on that page. Once you've found all of the letters on the SOCIAL FORTUNE side, flip the book and find the hidden letters on the SOCIAL FATE side. Once you've found all of the letters, write them in the boxes that follow and you'll reveal the Words of Wisdom.

Y

Fortune	Fortune	Fortune		Fortune	Fortune	Fortune		Fortune		Fortune	Fortune	Fortune	Fate	Fate	Fate
Pg 2	Pg 4	Pg 6		Pg 8	Pg 10	Pg 12		Pg 14		Pg 16	Pg 18	Pg 20	Pg 2	Pg 4	Pg 6

!

Fate	Fate	Fate	Fate	Fate	Fate	Fate
Pg 8	Pg 10	Pg 12	Pg 14	Pg 16	Pg 18	Pg 20

What About You?

So here's the deal. It may be easy to see (in this graphic novel) the moment when the characters make a choice that leads them down the road of SOCIAL FATE. It's always easier to see when others are doing something Unexpected for the situation. But what about you? If you found yourself in a similar situation, which road would you take? The road to SOCIAL FORTUNE or the road that leads to SOCIAL FATE? Take the journey with Kiko, JT, and Rin, and then think about your own journeys too!

By the way, ALL of us are working on developing and improving our Social Thinking and related social skills throughout our whole lives. No one should ever feel like they are done learning about how their behaviors affect others. Just ask your parents or teachers about how much they still have to think about what to do in certain social situations. We're pretty sure, if they're like us and everyone else, that at times they still get stuck trying to figure out what to do or say to stay on the road to SOCIAL FORTUNE.

But remember, being on the road to SOCIAL FATE happens to all of us at one time or another in our lives! Making mistakes and upsetting others, at times, is just what is called "being human." We know that people don't want to upset others most of the time, but it happens! When it does happen, use your problem solving skills.

This means you should think back to the choice you made that put you on the road to SOCIAL FATE. If a similar situation comes up again in the future, make the choice that will mostly likely put you on the road to SOCIAL FORTUNE. Why? Because this is the road that not only helps others to feel pretty good about you, but also helps you to feel good about yourself!

Remember, it is not a problem to make a mistake! It's only a problem when you don't learn from your mistakes!

FINAL TIP: If you landed on the road to SOCIAL FATE by accident – don't sweat it (meaning don't panic). One way to get back on the right road is to apologize to the person who might have been offended or hurt. Apologies are a way of letting others know that, although you made a mistake, you were thinking about them in a good way.

MEET THE CHARACTERS

JT

Rin

Kiko

SOCIAL FORTUNE

OR
SOCIAL FATE

A SOCIAL THINKING® GRAPHIC NOVEL MAP
FOR SOCIAL QUEST SEEKERS

WATCH THEIR DESTINIES UNFOLD BASED ON THE CHOICES THEY MAKE

Social FORTUNE—Been There, Know That

SOCIAL SITUATION: Participating in class discussion

Important: The behaviors listed below aren't in any particular order. For example, the first behavior in column one doesn't have to match the first feeling in column two and so on. We've put some circles on this first map to show you the connections in the story that go with this map.

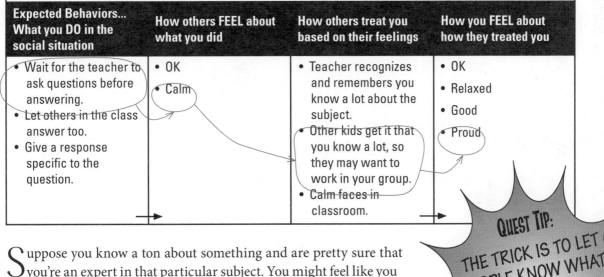

Expected Behaviors... What you DO in the social situation	How others FEEL about what you did	How others treat you based on their feelings	How you FEEL about how they treated you
• Wait for the teacher to ask questions before answering. • Let others in the class answer too. • Give a response specific to the question.	• OK • Calm	• Teacher recognizes and remembers you know a lot about the subject. • Other kids get it that you know a lot, so they may want to work in your group. • Calm faces in classroom.	• OK • Relaxed • Good • Proud

QUEST TIP:

THE TRICK IS TO LET PEOPLE KNOW WHAT YOU KNOW... WITHOUT TAKING OVER THE GROUP!

Suppose you know a ton about something and are pretty sure that you're an expert in that particular subject. You might feel like you really want the teacher and the other kids to get the facts right. But, here's the deal about being in a classroom. You are part of a group! Sometimes people know a lot, sometimes they know just a little; sometimes they're interested, and sometimes they're bored. That really doesn't matter because learning in a group requires thinking about others and figuring out the hidden rules of that situation. Kiko, in this case, realized he needed to think about others around him. Sure, he was bored and yes, he knew more than many of the kids, BUT...he decided not to let everyone know!

KIKO'S STRATEGY CODES:

1. FOR (**F**igure **O**ut **R**ules). Kiko knew the situation had obvious and hidden rules, and just because he knew more than anyone else, he didn't announce it. He figured out that he needed to wait for the question, then raise his hand and wait for the teacher to call on him. And, he figured out just the right amount of information to give when answering the question. Giving too much information (or everything he knew) would be unexpected for the situation.

2. MOBS (**M**oments **O**f **B**oredom **S**urvival). Kiko was probably bored on several occasions because he already knew the facts. But, he called on all of his inner strength to survive the boring moments. More on this later.

3. TAC (**T**hink **A**bout **C**hoices). In this case, he thought about what he would do to keep the teacher and classmates having OK thoughts and feeling calm. It made a difference because he was the one in the end who felt PROUD about himself.

OPTION: Flip the book upside down and read from the back to see what happens when Kiko makes a different choice. What road would you take in this example?

SOCIAL FORTUNE–Speak Nothin' but the Truth

SOCIAL SITUATION: Someone you like (or are friends with) does something different with their appearance.

Expected Behaviors... What you DO in the social situation	How others FEEL about what you did	How others treat you based on their feelings	How you FEEL about how they treated you
• Keep thoughts that are hurtful in your head. • Make supportive comments. • Face is relaxed or friendly.	• Calm • Supported	• May tell you that you are appreciated. • May want to spend more time with you.	• Appreciated • Happy

QUEST TIP: FIGURE OUT WHICH THOUGHTS SHOULD STAY IN YOUR HEAD.

So, you've always been told to be honest and state your opinions. That's true a lot of the time or when the truth doesn't hurt someone's feelings, but what about in this situation? JT had a thought and an opinion about his friend Rin's new hair cut. Did he NEED to say exactly what he was thinking? JT had to make a quick decision. He decided that it didn't really matter if he liked her hair or not because he just likes to be with her. This example is really tricky, but things like this happen all the time to everyone. Have a talk with your teacher or parents to get their views on whether it's always important to say what you think even if you might hurt someone you care about. This is probably one of the hardest hidden rules in the social world so take some time to talk about this with an adult you trust.

JT'S STRATEGY CODES:

1. FOR (**F**igure **O**ut the **R**ules). JT knew the hidden rule that it's not always important to tell exactly what you think about something, especially when it comes to a person's appearance. He was a definite SOCIAL THINKER in his choice-making because he thought about Rin's thoughts and feelings when he made his choice to comment.

2. FOTO (**F**ilter **O**pinions and **T**houghts **O**ften). This is one of the most powerful strategy codes known to humankind. The idea is that you have a filter in your brain, sorta like a pasta drainer (colander) or coffee filter or tightly woven fishing net. That filter is there to catch things that you THINK in your head but that shouldn't always come out of your mouth. You need to know that everyone in the world has thoughts that need to run through their brain filter and be stopped. It's a part of being a sensitive person. This is something that takes a lot of practice. Many adults are still working on making sure their filter is always ready.

3. TAC (**T**hink **A**bout **C**hoices). JT made a conscious choice to keep Rin having good thoughts and feeling calm. He stayed true to himself too because although he didn't like her hair, he does like her. He was able to make a comment that was honest and not harmful. He ended up feeling appreciated in the end.

OPTION: Keep going forward or flip the book upside down and read from the back to see what happens when JT makes a different choice. What road would you take in this example?

SOCIAL FORTUNE–Bored Outta My Brain
SOCIAL SITUATION: Being part of the learning group during a boring moment

Expected Behaviors... What you DO in the social situation	How others FEEL about what you did	How others treat you based on their feelings	How you FEEL about how they treated you
• Do the Social Fake • Don't let others know you are bored	• Calm • Good	• Teacher may notice you kept eyes/brain in the group	• Neutral • Calm

Let's face it. There are times at school and some moments with people and parents that are just plain boring. That's the way it is. But…how you deal with the boring moment is crucial. Kiko used something called the "Social Fake." It's a strategy lots of us use to keep our eyes and body in the group when it's important to do so. In this case, Kiko was bored and thought about plopping his head down on the desk and taking a little nap. When he was little, he was taught that it was important to always "pay attention." Now that he's older, it's time for him to use the Social Fake. Kiko was able to think about what the teacher was saying but also could check in and out without her knowing and feeling like he was rude.

QUEST TIP:
BORING MOMENTS?
USE THE SOCIAL FAKE.

KIKO'S STRATEGY CODES:

1. SF (**S**ocial **F**ake). Legend has it that humans have done the Social Fake for centuries. We just didn't always have the words to describe this very important strategy. It's simply a way to survive a moment that may be boring by acting like you're attending with your eyes and body. The reality is that your brain may wander for a split second or two but then "check back" with the other person. In that way, you don't seem like you're bored outta your brains, and the other person feels like you're part of the group.

2. FOTO (**F**ilter **O**pinions and **T**houghts **O**ften). Kiko was able to use his brain filter to catch his thought that he was really bored. Thoughts in your head shouldn't always come out of your mouth. You need to know that everyone in the world has thoughts that need to run through their brain filter and get stopped from proceeding to their mouths. It's a part of being a person. This is something that takes a lot of practice.

3. TAC (**T**hink **A**bout **C**hoices). Kiko certainly had choices here. He could have plopped his head down on the desk, pulled out a book from his backpack and read, played with his pencil or just checked out. BUT - he didn't do any of those things. Instead, he thought about his choices and decided to use the Social FAKE. Good choice.

OPTION: Keep going forward or flip the book upside down and read from the back to see what happens when Kiko makes a different choice. What road would you take in this example?

Social FORTUNE—It's Doomsday! (Or Is It?)
SOCIAL SITUATION: Time to finish homework

Expected Behaviors... What you DO in the social situation	How others FEEL about what you did	How others treat you based on their feelings	How you FEEL about how they treated you
• Think about the size of the problem • Take a deep breath and stay calm	• Proud • Relieved	• Encourage you • Leave you alone	• Calm • Proud

Surviving the world of homework and chores and just about everything else means we have to figure out the size of the problem right there staring us in the face and then figure out how to react in a way that matches up. Rin got it by THINKING first about how big the problem really was—size 3 out of 10—and then reacting in a smaller way. Nice work on her part because she wound up getting exactly what she wanted in the end. We often use a Size of the Problem Thermometer to help solve this quest. (Hint: There's one in the middle of this book. You'll see more about this on the SOCIAL FATE road for this social situation.)

QUEST TIP: MATCH IT UP – PROBLEM SIZE AND REACTION SIZE GO TOGETHER.

RIN'S STRATEGY CODES:

1. **MARP** (**M**inimize **A R**eaction to the **P**roblem). Probably seems like a no-brainer that a person's reaction should only be as big as the problem. The trick is actually keeping the reaction smaller. It can be tough and an ongoing struggle for Auto-Pilot Reactors, but it's possible! Rin used the strategy of thinking about the size of her problem by picturing a Problem Thermometer in her head and using it to decide the size of her current problem. Once she figured out it was a 3, she realized that her reaction should be smaller than a 3. This is important because people notice when the reaction is as big or bigger than the problem and that makes others feel uncomfortable. It takes some practice, but we all have to learn this skill, even parents and teachers!

2. **TAC** (**T**hink **A**bout **C**hoices). Rin did what Social Thinkers often do....she took a second to think about her choice because she knew that it would have an impact on her mom's thoughts and feelings. In this case, her mom had a really good thought about how Rin reacted and then Rin felt proud. That worked out well because her mom ended up encouraging her and Rin felt CALM in the end. Pretty cool how this cycle works!

OPTION: Take a look at what happened when Rin made a different choice by flipping the book upside down and backward. What road would you take in this example?

Social FORTUNE—Clue Me In!

SOCIAL SITUATION: Figuring out what to say to others

Expected Behaviors... What you DO in the social situation	How others FEEL about what you did	How others treat you based on their feelings	How you FEEL about how they treated you
• Use eyes, ears, and memory to make a smart guess about the people you are near • Get body and eyes into the group • Connect to their comments or questions	• Neutral • Calm • Relaxed	• May ask you questions • May look at you to acknowledge you are part of the group • May pay attention to you when you are speaking	• Good • OK • Included

QUEST TIP: MAKE A SMART GUESS!!

So, figuring out what to say to other people when you see them is sometimes hard. We get it! Many of us work on this our whole lives. But we've got a strategy that might help. Think of yourself as a social secret agent who uses your own special investigative tools (eyes, ears, and brain) to make a SMART GUESS. In the map above, JT listened to what the guys were saying and realized he could talk about their teacher even if he was not in the class. Another important point is that JT put his body in the group (meaning about an arm's length away from the others) to show them that he wanted to be a part of what was happening. Practice this with your family. Think about the person, look at what's going on, listen to what is being said, get your body in the group, and then make a smart guess about what to say or ask based on what you see and hear. **EXTRA TIP:** It's okay if you haven't ever done (or seen) the experience that the person is talking about to be able to say something. JT did it by just making a comment that connected to what the other guys were saying.

JT'S STRATEGY CODES:

1. SG (**S**mart **G**uess). JT used the strategy of making a Smart Guess. This is something that SOCIAL THINKERS rely on whenever they approach a group of people or even just one other person. Here's how it worked for JT. He saw some guys that he knew and was a little worried he wouldn't know what to say – but, he paid attention to what they were talking about and connected just by making a comment. Once he acted like he was interested in them, the other guys used their eyes, ears and brains to make a smart guess to figure out that JT was interested in anime.

2. TAC (**T**hink **A**bout **C**hoices). JT could have simply walked away when he first thought to himself, "I never know what to say to people," but he didn't. Instead he figured out that he could be a part of the group. He knew Kiko already, so he was able to get his body into the group and then start with a greeting to keep everyone having OK thoughts and neutral feelings. In the end, JT felt pretty good about his choice.

3. FOR (**F**igure **O**ut the **R**ules). The hidden rule in this case is that moving away from a group makes people wonder why you've left. They may think you don't like them or that you think you're too good for the group. It may make you more comfortable, but it may also make others uncomfortable.

OPTION: You know the routine. You can keep going to the next story or flip the book and see what happens when JT makes different choices. Don't forget to think about what road you would take.

Social FORTUNE–Huh?

SOCIAL SITUATION: Getting help in the classroom

Expected Behaviors... What you DO in the social situation	How others FEEL about what you did	How others treat you based on their feelings	How you FEEL about how they treated you
• Realize you need help because you're frustrated • Raise your hand (wait to be called on) • Ask for help (or ask for more information)	• Relieved	• Might ask you for help • You'll get help from the person	• Calm • Proud • Relaxed

Getting help sometimes seems like it's a really big deal, but it doesn't have to be. A lot of us wish we could figure out how to do everything on our own, but being human makes that impossible. We ALL have to ask for help sometimes. Really, you CAN'T know everything! We understand that it's sometimes annoying to not know what to do, but we've found that most often if you need help, others do too. Kiko figured out he needed help and then asked for it.

QUEST TIP: WE ALL NEED IT SOMETIMES... HELP!

KIKO'S STRATEGY CODES:

1. INCH (**IN**ner **C**oach **H**elp). This is an important strategy for almost everyone. The inner coach is simply that internal silent voice in your brain that encourages you to "keep going" or "stay calm" or gives other supporting words. It's actually just YOU or your own voice telling your brain to hang in there! Kiko used his inner coach by thinking, "Keep your cool here...I only need a little help, but still I need to ask for help."

2. FOR (**F**igure **O**ut the **R**ules). Kiko was brilliant in this social situation. He knew that in this math class the obvious rule is to ask for help from the teacher when you don't know what to do. In some classes, the hidden rule is that you ask a peer before you ask the teacher, but Kiko already knew the rule for this class. Another obvious (and sometimes hidden) rule is that you raise your hand and look at the teacher and then wait to be called on before you ask for help. Good thinking on his part because it turns out that lots of other kids needed help too!

3. TAC (**T**hink **A**bout **C**hoices). Kiko could have yelled out, "I don't get it!", but he thought about how others would react, including the teacher. He was a SOCIAL THINKER and made the right choice to keep others feeling neutral and calm.

OPTION: So, flip the book and take a peek to see what happens when Kiko is an Auto-Pilot Reactor.

PROUD

Excellent! I avoided the blurt!

Rin, you can answer the next one.

CALM

Finally, I got to answer one.

WHAT SHE DOES

That's good, Rin didn't blurt out.

Oops! I checked out for a minute, but Mr. V is looking at Amelia. So, not my turn.

So, what did you find?

Hmm...wonder what's for lunch?

Oh....he's looking at me so I guess I get to answer this one.

Let's talk about the class online assignment.

Focus... don't blurt!

C'mon Rin, avoid the blurt!

Social FORTUNE–You Talkin' to Me?

SOCIAL SITUATION – Classroom lesson when you know the answer

Expected Behaviors... What you DO in the social situation	How others FEEL about what you did	How others treat you based on their feelings	How you FEEL about how they treated you
• Think about staying focused	• Calm	• May give you the next turn	• Proud
• Use eyes to figure out who the teacher is talking to	• Relieved	• Smile	• Relieved
• Keep thoughts in your head until it's your turn to answer		• Doesn't nag you	• Calm

QUEST TIP: YOU'VE GOTTA KNOW WHEN IT'S YOUR TIME TO SHINE!

When you were really young, teachers would simply call out your name if they wanted you to talk or answer a question. But as you get older, teachers use their eyes to indicate to you when it's your time to show your knowledge. If people forget or don't use their eyes to figure out when it's their turn to speak, they might "blurt." Blurting happens when one person talks over the top of another person's words when it's not her turn. In this story, Rin stopped looking at the teacher for a bit and zoned out (or started thinking about something else for a second or two). BUT, Rin knew she had a history of blurting and that she needed to use her eyes to figure out WHO the teacher expected to answer the question. When she avoided blurting out the answer, everyone around her felt pretty good and treated her in a more positive way.

RIN'S STRATEGY CODES:

1. **NOBZ** (**No B**lurting **Z**one). We all blurt sometimes, but it's something to try to always avoid in the classroom. Rin combined the INCH strategy (see below) with her knowledge that the classroom is a No Blurting Zone. The way to avoid blurting is to use your eyes to figure out who the other person is speaking to and then decide whether or not it's you. If it's not, don't respond until it's your turn.

2. **INCH** (**In**ner **C**oach **H**elp). INCH is explained a little more in the last map about asking for help so you can look back at those strategy codes for more info. In this story, Rin used her inner coach (her own voice that encourages her) to remind her brain to focus on the speaker and keep her thoughts in her head. As you can see, she lost her focus for just a minute, but then she used INCH again to remind herself to wait until the teacher was looking at and thinking about her.

3. **TAC** (**T**hink **A**bout **C**hoices). So Rin has a little problem with blurting out the answers. After all, she usually knows them. The problem is that other kids never seem to get the chance to show their knowledge too. In this story, Rin remembered to avoid the blurt, and that kept everyone thinking and feeling calm. She was the winner in the end too because she felt proud that she monitored her own behavior and made the right choice.

OPTION: How about you? Are you sometimes a blurter? It takes practice, but you can use strategies like Rin did to stay on the road to Social Fortune!

SOCIAL FORTUNE–My Way or the Highway!
SOCIAL SITUATION – Working in a small group

Expected Behaviors... What you DO in the social situation	How others FEEL about what you did	How others treat you based on their feelings	How you FEEL about how they treated you
• Think about working as part of the group • Remind your brain to be flexible and do what the group is doing • Think about the size of the problem, and if it's a small one…let it be!	• Relieved • Okay • Calm	• May want to work with you again • May let you choose which part of the project to do • Friendly faces • Friendly words	• Okay • Calm

Sometimes it seems like your idea is the only one that could possibly be right. And sometimes, you might have the best idea….but not always. Whenever people work in groups, they have to learn to be flexible in their thinking. By the way, none of us can avoid working in groups all the time… it's a reality of school and work. When one person in the group gets STUCK on doing everything her way, we call her a rigid thinker. Rigid thinkers have a very hard time seeing anyone else's way of doing things. JT is a very rigid thinker and really hates to work in groups. He knows that his ideas are likely the best BUT he's also practicing his choice-making as a SOCIAL THINKER. He was able to realize that he had to figure out how to be a flexible thinker in order to finish the project. It wasn't easy, but JT had to tell his brain that "this isn't a big problem" and in this situation, "I can be flexible." Once he was able to flex with the group idea, everyone felt better about working together. In the end, JT felt OK too.

QUEST TIP: LEARN TO BE A FLEXIBLE THINKER.

JT'S STRATEGY CODES:

1. FLEX-T (FLEXible Thinking). If we could pick one strategy code that would help kids everywhere, it would be this one. Learning to be a flexible thinker is a matter of survival in social situations. We're not saying it's easy and we know it takes practice—but flexible thinking just means that you're working to see that there's more than ONE way to solve a problem.

2. MARP (Minimize A Reaction to the Problem). We reviewed this strategy earlier in Rin's struggle with her homework, and now JT is using the same strategy for working in a group. He had to tell himself that trying someone else's idea wasn't a big problem.

3. TAC (Think About Choices). JT was able to understand that his choice to be a flexible thinker was really important for the group to finish the project. Because of his choice, the group finished and everyone felt OK in the end.

OPTION: Yikes! JT made a different choice on the road to SOCIAL FATE. Flip the book to see.

SOCIAL FORTUNE–Who Changed the Rules?

SOCIAL SITUATION – Break time

Expected Behaviors... What you DO in the social situation	How others FEEL about what you did	How others treat you based on their feelings	How you FEEL about how they treated you
• Think about what's expected in this situation • Use your thinking to coach yourself • Use your eyes, body, and words to join the group	• Relaxed • Okay • Calm	• May stay around you • Might include you in their discussion • May look friendly	• Included • Good

It's just something we can't control—the social RULES keep changing as we get older. For example, when Kiko was younger, it was OK to play with his toys at break time, but now that he's older…the rules are different. It doesn't mean that he can't play at home—it's that it's EXPECTED that he'll use his eyes and brain to figure out what everyone else is doing during break and join in at times. In this case, Kiko used his brain power to think about what to do and then coached himself with his thinking to say "hey" to Rin. Even though Kiko really wanted to do his own thing, he made the choice to do his best to blend with what others were doing. Oh…by the way, Kiko played with his toys when he got home from school. Good choice!

QUEST TIP: RULES CHANGE – SO SHOULD YOU!

KIKO'S STRATEGY CODES:

1. **RCA** (**R**ules **C**hange with **A**ge). This is just a fact, and Kiko remembered that what was OK at a younger age is no longer OK now that he's older. The cool thing about this is that even though the rules change for what's expected and unexpected at school and around others, that doesn't mean that it's the same for alone time at home. Kiko was still able to play with his stuff at home. RCA is also considered a hidden rule (read below).

2. **FOR** (**F**ind **O**ut the Hidden **R**ules). This is very much a part of knowing about the RCA. In fact, in this story Kiko figured out the hidden rule that playing with toys during break at school is unexpected for guys his age. By doing this, he kept everyone around him feeling OK and calm.

3. **INCH** (**IN**ner **C**oach **H**elp). INCH was already explained in a couple of other maps, but in this story Kiko used his inner coach to remind himself that the rules for what's expected at his age have changed. He also used INCH to remind himself that going into the group was OK because he already knew Rin. Just like the rest of us - Kiko knew that it feels good to be included by others at times. So, Kiko knew what he needed to do to make that happen. He made the choice to focus on what his peers were doing and that encouraged people to include him in the group.

OPTION: Things didn't go as well for Kiko on the SOCIAL FATE road. Flip the book to see or just keep reading.

Social FORTUNE—Know When To Take A Detour

SOCIAL SITUATION – Sharing ideas/opinions

Expected Behaviors...What you DO in the social situation	How others FEEL about what you did	How others treat you based on their feelings	How you FEEL about how they treated you
• Think about what's expected in the situation • When you realize you said something that may offend someone else, stop talking about it and change the topic! • Make comments that are more in line with what the other person may want to talk about or say nothing at all.	• Okay, but initially irritated • Calm • Fine, let things go	• May continue to talk to you after you initially irritated them • May continue to include you in the group • May just leave you alone	• Relieved • Okay • Neutral

QUEST TIP: THINK – HOW DO I GET OUT OF THIS MESS?

So, we all have opinions and sometimes our opinions are based on feelings ("I don't like that because it seems smelly") or based on fact ("Science tells us to avoid too much salt"). In this case, JT definitely had an opinion or two about what his peer was eating. BUT—he took a few seconds to realize the other guy did not share the same opinion as JT. Smartly, JT realized that he needed to take a detour away from talking about his dislike of eggs and shift his comments to something else. He was really smart to do this because the guy was hanging out with a girl and the two of them could make him feel really bad if JT kept trying to push his opinion about eggs. When two people are made uncomfortable by what one person is doing, sometimes they gang up on that person and make him feel really bad for his mistake.

JT'S STRATEGY CODES:

1. TAD (**T**ake **A D**etour). This defensive move is very powerful. Sometimes you find yourself in a social situation and realize that you had better get out of it, make a turn, or find a new way! It's kind of like when you're in a car or bus and there's something in the road blocking you. You have to take a detour. That's what happened here to JT. He was about to go down the bumpy road of scolding his classmate and suddenly realized he needed to make a detour quickly to avoid a social crash. Good thing JT had this defensive strategy in his bag because he was able to combine it with FOTO and INCH to stay on the road to Social Fortune.

2. FOTO (**F**ilter **O**pinions and **T**houghts **O**ften). JT used his brain filter to catch his thought that the eggs were gross and that, in his opinion, only eggs from free-range chickens should be eaten. Good move on his part because that's his opinion and not worth causing a problem with the other kid.

3. INCH (**IN**ner **C**oach **H**elp). JT used his inner coach to remind himself about FOTO and he decided to just "let it go." He could have shifted his comments to say something else but in this case, he decided to say nothing. This little bit of encouragement was enough to avoid a problem.

4. He used **FOR** and **RCA** too!

OPTION: What would you have done in this example?

PROBLEM SOLVING THERMOMETER

Size of the Problem

BIG Problems (8-10):

_____

_____

_____

_____

MEDIUM Problems (4-7):

_____

_____

_____

_____

_____

SMALL Problems (1-3) :

_____

_____

_____

NOT a Problem (0):

_____

_____

_____

_____

Feelings and Responding in a smaller way to medium and small size problems

_____

_____

_____

_____

Feelings and Responses for
MEDIUM Problems (2-4):

_____

_____

_____

_____

Feelings and Responses for
SMALL Problems (0-1):

_____

_____

Not a Problem (0):

_____

_____

_____

_____

10

9

8 FBI

7

6

5

4 ESP

3

2

1

0

MEDIUM Reaction

SMALL Reaction

Feel it **B**ig on the **I**nside (**FBI**) but **E**xpress it **S**maller when in **P**ublic (**ESP**)

"With *Social Fortune or Social Fate*, Pamela Crooke and Michelle Garcia Winner promote the idea of social competence (not just social skills) in a way that incorporates research in the areas of visual learning and cognitive behavioral interventions. In addition, their use of the graphic novel as a platform to translate social concepts into complex behavioral repertoires takes a popular medium and uses it in a, potentially, very productive way."

Dr. Peter Gerhardt
Director, McCarton Upper School
New York, New York

"Love the emotion meters, thought and speech bubbles and graphics as a way to help students incorporate and internalize what they have learned from social-behavior mapping and hidden curriculum lessons. This is a great way for teens to learn about their own and others' Social Thinking."

Lydia Garcia Liu, M.S.
Speech Language Pathologist
Tucson, Arizona

"Cool! The illustrations would appeal to ages 12-17. The facial expressions show what they are feeling. When you flip the book it's like a replay on a social situation."

Tyler Bozetski
High school sophomore, age 16

"Once again Garcia Winner and Crooke have zeroed in on a critical social thinking concept that many of our kids struggle with: making choices and predicting the corresponding consequences. Through clever organization, the authors present 10 social scenarios in anime-style cartoon strips where the characters make their choices and, on the opposite page, discuss the consequences of that choice. Each social scenario begins with a good choice (Fortune) or unexpected choice (Fate). The outcome hinges on perspective taking before making a choice. *Social Fortune or Social Fate* is a must have in the Social Thinking toolbox. Our kids are really enjoying discussing the scenarios and relating them to their own life choices."

David Myford, MSW, LSW
School Social Worker
Communication Development Program
Southwest Cook County Cooperative for Special Education

Social Fortune

or

Social Fate

A SOCIAL THINKING® GRAPHIC NOVEL MAP
FOR SOCIAL QUEST SEEKERS

WATCH THEIR DESTINIES UNFOLD BASED ON THE CHOICES THEY MAKE

Social
Thinking jr..com

Social Thinking Publishing, San Jose, California
www.socialthinking.com

SOCIAL FORTUNE
OR
SOCIAL FATE

A SOCIAL THINKING® GRAPHIC NOVEL MAP FOR SOCIAL QUEST SEEKERS

WATCH THEIR DESTINIES UNFOLD BASED ON THE CHOICES THEY MAKE

Pamela Crooke and

Michelle Garcia Winner

Social
ThinkinGr.com

Social Thinking Publishing, San Jose, California
www.socialthinking.com

Social Fortune or Social Fate
A Social Thinking© Graphic Novel Map for Social Quest Seekers

Pamela Crooke and Michelle Garcia Winner

Illustrated by www.tiger-arts.com

Graphic Design by Elizabeth A Blacker, elizabethblacker@me.com

Library of Congress Control Number: 2010935012

ISBN: 978-0-9825231-5-5

Social Thinking Publishing
3031 Tisch Way, Suite 800
San Jose, CA 95128
Phone: (877) 464-9278
Fax: (408) 557-8594

This book is printed and bound in Tennessee by Mighty Color Printing.
Books may be ordered online at www.socialthinking.com.

To learn more about Social Thinking® concepts for adolescents, please explore:

Thinking About You Thinking About Me, 2nd edition

Social Behavior Mapping

Socially Curious and Curiously Social (a book for teens to read)

Worksheets! For Teaching Social Thinking and Related Social Skills

….and many more titles.

www.socialthinking.com

SOCIAL FATE TABLE OF CONTENTS

SOCIAL FORTUNE OR SOCIAL FATE

Don't Skip Over This Part....

We know you're tempted to flip to the graphic pages in this book, but we'd like you to know about a few hidden things before you start. You have some choices about how you read this book, and we want to give you all the options first. This book has graphics, maps, hidden letters, emotion meters, and a couple of other things for you to discover. So, hang in there and read the following pages—it will make your quest a better one.

You should know right up front that this graphic novel is all about CHOICES. Have you ever thought about how many choices we all make in a day? It's about a zillion! You know, little things like how long do I brush my teeth this morning, or should I try to find the match to this sock, or where should I put my game control so that my little brother won't touch it? And choices aren't only at home and not just with things. We make choices all day long about what to say (or not to say) to people, whether or not to get into a group, when to ramp up (get super angry), and when to cool down (get relaxed and calm).

Some choices don't seem to matter much, like matching a sock. But other choices are pretty important, especially ones in social situations. That's what this book is about—social choices in social situations and why they matter. But first we've gotta give you the scoop on what we mean by social situations.

You Can't Avoid Them...They're Everywhere

Have you ever noticed that every place you are during the day has a different set of things that you're expected to do and even words you're expected to say? And, what's expected is based on where you are at that moment and the people who are around you. Each time you're supposed to use a different set of social behaviors based on what's happening around you, that's called a social situation. Here are some examples to make this a little clearer. These are just examples, so what's expected of you in your situation will probably be a little different.

Social Situation #1 = Having dinner with the family at home

Place: **Home**
Time: **Evening**
Who's there: **Maybe some or all family members**
What's expected: **Depends on the family. Every family has a set of "rules" that are expected during mealtimes. Some might be that you sit at the table, eat your meal with a fork and spoon, clean up after yourself, and on and on. There's a range of what's expected because every family is different.**

Social Situation #2 = Eating lunch at school

Place: **School**
Time: **Middle of the day**
Who's there: **Kids at school**
What's expected: **Hang out, eat lunch using hands or fork depending on what's for lunch, walk around, read, and on and on. It depends on the school and your age, but every school has a set of "rules" that kids are supposed to figure out for lunch break.**

Social Situation #3 = Asking a question in class

Place: School

Time: Most of the time when in class

Who's there: Kids at school and teachers too

What's expected: Depends on the class, but many teachers want you to raise your hand and wait for them to call on you before you ask your question.

IMPORTANT: Every one of us has to figure out or calculate what the RULES are in every social situation!

Rules Are Sometimes Hidden!

In every social situation, there are things that people do and say that are OK (expected) and NOT OK (unexpected) for that exact time and in that particular place. In fact, every time any of us walks into a new social situation, one of the first things we do is try to figure out the rules of that particular situation. We all have to do this! Every single one of us! Sometimes the rules are super easy and clear, and sometimes they are "unspoken" or "hidden." Here are a couple of examples:

Social Situation = Passing other kids in the halls at school

Obvious rules: People are expected to walk (not crawl or slither or roll down the hall). People carry their own stuff (rather than grab others' backpacks or things). And on and on…

Hidden rules: It's also expected that kids will accidentally bump into one another in a crowded space. Kids may do things in the halls that aren't OK in class (talk in a loud voice volume, run, etc) but are OK here. And on and on…

Each social situation has a set of obvious rules and hidden rules, and it sometimes takes a little practice to figure them out. Once you've figured out the hidden rules or what's expected and unexpected in that situation, it's time to make choices.

The cool thing about this is that once we've figured out the rules, we get to make choices about what we say and do or what NOT to say and do. The trick is to know what's expected and then make the choice to do just that! Next, we'll look at some types of ways that people make choices in social situations. Take a minute to think about the choice-maker that best describes YOU. Keep in mind that every choice someone makes around others affects how those people feel about the behavior they observe.

1. Auto-Pilot Reactor:

This person forgets to think about the social situation and so puts his brain on auto-pilot. He doesn't really think too much about the choices he makes and reacts really quickly or without considering how his actions or words might affect others. This person often ends up really confused or angry because his quick reactions cause others to be hurt or angry or annoyed. You'll see some examples of this in the book.

2. Option Resister:

Well, sometimes a person actually does take the time to think about the situation but thinks her way is the only way. This is the kind of choice-making where the person takes a minute to figure out the social situation but forgets to (or doesn't) consider that her choices affect others. In other words, she just thinks about what she thinks is best or easiest or more comfortable for her. There are many examples of this in the book as well.

3. Coin Flipper:

So let's say a person doesn't want to think and instead really wants to rely on chance or the flip of a coin to help him make social choices. There are a couple of problems with this option. First of all, it would be kinda awkward with a coin…walking around the halls and at home flipping and flipping and then making choices based on that. Another problem is that it would only give a person a 50% or so success rate. Not the best idea. There are no Coin Flippers in this book and we hope to never see one.

4. Social Thinker:

This person uses his brain to THINK and then figure out the social situation and use a strategy code (we'll talk about these later) to know what to say or do. This graphic novel has plenty of examples of this type of thinking. You'll see the characters use Social Thinking to figure out what to do in the social situation.

In this book, three characters (Kiko, Rin, and JT) find themselves in a whole bunch of social situations where they have to make choices about what to do and say (or not say). When they do what's expected, their journey follows a map that takes them on the road of SOCIAL FORTUNE. If they do what's unexpected for the situation, the map leads them down the road of SOCIAL FATE. So now we need to explain what we mean by the roads and this special type of map.

Maps and Roads

You know about typical maps, but the map in this book is different. You'll see that the three characters find themselves using this map during every situation. We call it a Social Behavior Map. You'll learn more about it in the next few paragraphs, but the easiest way is to think of it as a map that has two parts. As we said before, if a person makes choices that are expected for that social situation, he is sent down the road to Social Fortune. If she makes choices that are unexpected for the social situation, she ends up on the road to Social Fate. Here's the cool thing. You'll get to see each of the characters make choices that lead him or her down both roads—Social Fortune and Social Fate! You'll see how things can really change for the characters based on what they choose.

Here's how the map works. It all starts with a social situation. Remember, a social situation is just about any time we're around others and there are rules about what to say or do.

Social Behavior Map

This map is a little different because it goes in a straight line. It starts in the left box and moves to each of the boxes to the right. How a person uses this map determines whether he (or she) goes on a road of Social Fortune or on a road of Social Fate. Take a look at the FIRST box in the road below.

1. What you do affects how another person feels

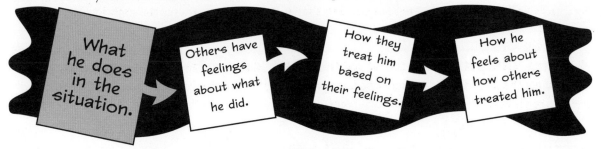

So you can see that the first step on the road is WHAT HE DOES in a social situation. This is where the characters in this book (or you) make a CHOICE about what social action they will take. It could be the movement they do with their bodies, their facial expression, or the words they say or don't say. You can see by the road below that the first box leads directly to the fact that others will have thoughts and feelings about what the person did or said (from the first box). There's an example of what we mean coming up next.

2. Others have feelings about what you do

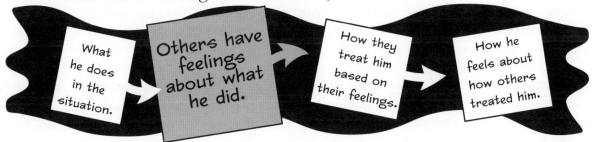

Here's an example:

Social Situation = Bedtime and mom tells Kiko to turn off the TV

What he did = Said "Yeah, OK mom." And then turned off the TV.

Well it's pretty obvious that Kiko's mom would have some sort of thought about how Kiko reacted to her request. In this case, his mom had a good or positive thought about what Kiko said and did. It's

the same for the rest of us. When we do or say something in a social situation, people have thoughts about it AND those thoughts are connected to a feeling! That's why you see the Emotion Meter right next to the mom's thoughts.

3. How people feel about your behavior affects how they treat you

Ok, you get the idea, right? But now let's keep going down the map a little further. The thoughts and feelings of others around us pretty much control how they treat us in that social situation. Take a look at the third box below.

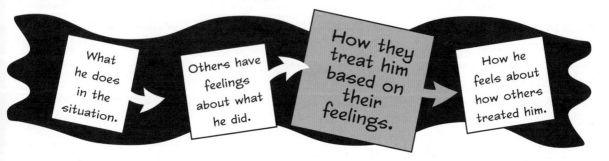

So Mom is feeling calm (which is always a good thing). And because she's calm, she'll react in a way that is calm too. For example, she might say something like, "Thanks for listening," or she might walk away and not nag Kiko to get going. "Avoiding the nag" is a huge accomplishment on his part!!

4. How people treat you affects how you feel about yourself

Finally, the last piece of the map is how Kiko feels about how the other person treated him. This is where you'll see more emotion meters in the book.

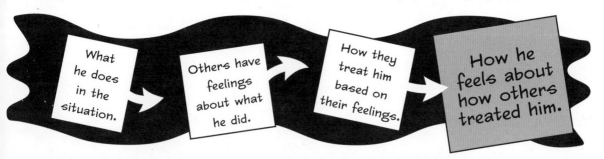

In this case, he can't help but feel "calm" or "relaxed" or even "happy" about the way his mom treated him.

Social Situation = Bedtime and mom tells Kiko to turn off the TV

What he did = Said "Yeah, OK mom." And then turned off the TV.

Mom's thoughts   Mom's feeling = Calm

CALM

How mom treated him: No nagging today!

How Kiko felt about avoiding the nag:

RELAXED

EMOTION METERS

PROUD

OKAY

FURIOUS

You'll see these meters all through the book. They're really important because the choices that Rin, Kiko, and JT make always leave others around them with a feeling or emotion. When the arrow faces to the left, it means that the person feels "good" or "fantastic" or "proud" or another positive emotion. When the arrow is in the middle, like in the example above, the person feels "neutral" or "calm" or "OK." When the arrow points more to the right, where the meter gets darker, the person feels a more negative emotion like "angry" or "annoyed" or "furious." It's the same for all of us and for you—whenever we say or do something in a social situation, we leave others with a thought and an emotion. That's why the second box on the map shows that others have thoughts and feelings connected to what he or she did.

Realize how fast this all happens!!!

You can see by the map that it all starts with the choice that our characters make in the social situation. Now, here's something important for real life: it only takes about one or two seconds to move along this map!

Expected and Unexpected behaviors: 2 sides to social behavior mapping

So that's the main idea about the map. But like any map, there's more than one route to take. This map has two roads. The first is the road of SOCIAL FORTUNE. That's the road Kiko took above. It most often has a pretty good ending for our characters because what happens along the way ends up with the person feeling pretty good about themselves. The road of SOCIAL FORTUNE is sometimes called the *Expected* road because the characters figure out what to do in that social situation and do what's expected in that time and place to keep others feeling OK or good or even great!

The other road, or the road of SOCIAL FATE, is often called the *Unexpected* road because the characters make a choice about what to do in that social situation that ends up being not so great because people get upset and treat them in a way they don't like.

Here's an example of the two roads side by side:

Social Situation: Bedtime and mom asks him to turn off the TV

Road of Social FORTUNE		Road of Social FATE
(Expected Road)		*(Unexpected Road)*

Fortune side	Question	Fate side
Says "Okay"	1. What he does in this specific situation	Says "NO" or just ignores her
CALM	2. Others' thoughts and feelings about what he did	ANGRY or ANNOYED
Mom says "Thanks" and he avoids the Nag	3. How they treated him based on those feelings	Mom yells or nags or takes away TV time
RELAXED or GOOD	4. How he feels about how she treated him	ANGRY or FRUSTRATED

So here's your first choice!

You can read this comic in a few different ways. If you read the Fortune side first and then the Fate side second, you'll see how all three characters are Social Thinkers and are able to take the road to SOCIAL FORTUNE. If you flip the book over and read the Fate side, you'll see what we mean by the power of "choice." This is where characters make different choices and end up on the road to SOCIAL

FATE. You'll see "Auto-Pilot Reactors" and "Option Resisters" on almost every page. But, you also have a third way to read the book. You can read the graphic story and then flip it over and read what happens when the character makes a different choice. The social situation is exactly the same (top four pictures) on the road to SOCIAL FORTUNE or SOCIAL FATE. What sends the character down one road or the other is the choice the character makes in the picture after the top four where it says "what he/she does." It's amazing to think that one little choice makes such a BIG difference in what happens in the end—but it does! So, it doesn't really matter which way you decide to read this book. It's up to you. Oh, by the way, your parents and teachers may learn a thing or two from this book, but you'll have to teach them how to use it. Most don't know a whole lot about graphic novel type books—they likely won't have a clue.

3 REALLY IMPORTANT THINGS YOU NEED TO KNOW!

1 THINKING ABOUT WHAT PEOPLE THINK ABOUT YOU

So the thing is – we think about each other even when we are not talking. We think about each other when we are just sitting in the same class or passing each other in the hall. People remember when others make them feel comfortable and they remember when people make them feel uncomfortable. In fact, people are more likely to remember when people make them feel upset or uncomfortable. Think about your own social memory. You probably can remember pretty clearly when someone did something to you that made you feel upset. When we are comfortable with a person, we are most likely having normal or good thoughts about that person. When a person makes us feel upset or stressed, we are most likely having uncomfortable or weird thoughts about that person. Here's the deal. The thoughts we have about a person have a direct connection to how we treat him or her. Most of us treat people ok/well when we have good thoughts about them and we are more likely to treat others badly when we have uncomfortable thoughts about them! The same goes for other people; they are likely to treat you the best when they have good thoughts about you and more likely to treat you the worst when they have weird or uncomfortable thoughts about you.

When someone does a "behavior" that causes an uncomfortable or weird thought, people usually call it a "problem behavior." So let's talk about problems!

2 THE SIZE OF THE PROBLEM

Some problems just happen and others are caused by people doing things that make others uncomfortable. But just because we call it a "problem" does not mean we should think of it as a catastrophe! Problems come in different sizes and not all problems require us to solve them with the same urgency or importance. Some problems really are quite small (like size 1,2, or 3) and are sometimes called "glitches." A glitch might be something like breaking your pencil lead or bumping a person by accident. Moderate to medium size problems (size 4, 5, 6 or 7) could be something like losing

your cell phone or tcalling someone a jerk! A big problem (size 8, 9 or 10) is one that upsets a lot of people and usually causes physical or money problems. This kind of problem is like when someone in your family gets in a car accident or a parent loses his or her job or there's a big natural disaster (like an earthquake or hurricane that comes close to you)! It is important to figure out how big a problem really is, because if you over-react to any size of problem, others can feel awkward, uncomfortable, or just plain annoyed. A big reaction to a problem means you're blasting your emotions in a really huge way. So the question is…How much emotion should you let fly out when you're really upset and how much is supposed to stay in? That's the next thing we need to talk about!

3 EMOTION EXPRESSION COMPRESSION

You already know that four-year-olds can go from super upset to goofy-happy. But something happens when we all get older – we are supposed to get better at controlling how we express our emotions especially when out in public, like at school. Social rules and expectations change with age and we all have to figure that out. This doesn't mean we don't have emotions! We can still get upset or really happy when we are at school, it is just expected that we down-play our feelings so that people perceive us to be relatively calm even when we are upset! We call this Emotion Expression Compression, or in everyday words – *Feel it Big on the Inside but Express it Smaller when in Public* (FBI-ESP). By the time we are in upper elementary school or beyond, others are more comfortable when feelings come out in "little bursts" rather than a blast of emotion. So, here's an example: If Kyle is really, really mad – others around him feel okay if he shows that he's a little irritated. But, if Kyle blows his emotions like a volcano, then others around him are uncomfortable with the lava flow of anger and now he's created another problem with them. Or, if Chandra thinks something is hilarious in class, her best bet (or best choice in this case) is to just smile or laugh a little rather than launch into a crazy laughing fit.

FBI-ESP: (**F**eel it **B**ig on the **I**nside but **E**xpress it **S**maller when in **P**ublic.) One strategy people use when they are feeling really big emotions on the inside and know they need to keep the size of their expression smaller on the outside is to take a couple of deep breathes when feeling really upset and then think about the fact that others will have really uncomfortable thoughts if they emit a burst of emotion in public.

We teach little kids that the size of the problem is supposed to match pretty closely to the emotions others see coming from them. So, if someone is having a size 5 problem, then it is OK for that little kid to show a size 5 reaction, which means they are acting pretty upset. But, like we said earlier, kids in upper elementary school and all the way into adulthood are supposed to play down their reactions to problems. So if they have a size 5 problem, they are supposed to stay pretty calm (like a size 1,2,3 response) while trying to repair their problem. An example of repairing would be that the kid explains the problem while keeping his voice and face mostly calm.

WARNING: Big negative reactions (looking/acting really upset) will make your teachers and other kids upset too and then you've got a whole new set of problems because everyone is feeling their own emotions because of your big reaction. An example might be if Antonio has

a big 'ol temper tantrum in the classroom. The teacher might feel frazzled, concerned, angry, disappointed, distracted or just plain annoyed. The other students may feel frustrated, threatened, embarrassed or irritated at Antonio. Ugh. This cycle of emotions just isn't good for anyone around Antonio. So you see…these emotions are really powerful and that's why we're giving you a big "heads-up" (meaning pay attention) so you'll know what to do the next time you get into a situation where a reaction might happen.

IMPORTANT: We know that sometimes things happen and you just need a good cry or yell. We also understand that you might need to talk with someone to help you figure out the size of your problem or why your emotions feel so huge. So, if it feels like your emotional volcano is always ready to blow no matter where you are, then you should ask someone in your family or a teacher/counselor at school to help. All of us, including adults, still have to think about FBI-ESP and they might have some strategies to help you.

 CHECK OUT THE PROBLEM SOLVING THERMOMETER AND FBI-ESP STRATEGY in the middle of this book. It's a reminder that your reaction needs to be smaller than the size of the problem itself!

Social Behavior Maps, Quest Tips, and Strategy Codes

After you read the graphic story on the left side of the page, you'll see a map on the right side. Remember, the beginning of the book showed a visual map that had four squares. This is exactly that same map, but we've filled it in for you. You'll see the social situation at the top of the page and then four columns. These columns are the same as the four map squares. These boxes have a Quest Tip and Strategy Codes. The Quest Tips talk a little about what happened in the social situation. Twelve different Strategy Codes show what each of the characters did during the journey to SOCIAL FORTUNE. You probably already noticed the strategy codes that are listed on the insides of both covers. If you didn't, you can take a look at them now or just wait to see them while you are reading the graphic stories.

Hidden Letters

Each page that has a comic story has a hidden letter somewhere in the graphics. Once you find all 20, you'll be able to put them together to decode the Words of Wisdom in the spaces below. To see an example, go to the graphic story on page Fortune/2. The hidden letter "Y" on this one is pretty obvious because it's on the boy's shirt in the third picture. The rest of the hidden letters won't be quite so easy. In fact, some are kinda tricky.

Start at the beginning of the SOCIAL FORTUNE side of the book. When you find each letter, write it on a sheet of paper or on that page. Once you've found all of the letters on the SOCIAL FORTUNE side, flip the book and find the hidden letters on the SOCIAL FATE side. Once you've found all of the letters, write them in the boxes that follow and you'll reveal the Words of Wisdom.

Y

| Fortune Pg 2 | Fortune Pg 4 | Fortune Pg 6 | | Fortune Pg 8 | Fortune Pg 10 | Fortune Pg 12 | | Fortune Pg 14 | | Fortune Pg 16 | Fortune Pg 18 | Fortune Pg 20 | Fate Pg 2 | Fate Pg 4 | Fate Pg 6 |

!

| Fate Pg 8 | Fate Pg 10 | Fate Pg 12 | Fate Pg 14 | Fate Pg 16 | Fate Pg 18 | Fate Pg 20 |

What About You?

So here's the deal. It may be easy to see (in this graphic novel) the moment when the characters make a choice that leads them down the road of SOCIAL FATE. It's always easier to see when others are doing something Unexpected for the situation. But what about you? If you found yourself in a similar situation, which road would you take? The road to SOCIAL FORTUNE or the road that leads to SOCIAL FATE? Take the journey with Kiko, JT, and Rin, and then think about your own journeys too!

By the way, ALL of us are working on developing and improving our Social Thinking and related social skills throughout our whole lives. No one should ever feel like they are done learning about how their behaviors affect others. Just ask your parents or teachers about how much they still have to think about what to do in certain social situations. We're pretty sure, if they're like us and every-one else, that at times they still get stuck trying to figure out what to do or say to stay on the road to SOCIAL FORTUNE.

But remember, being on the road to SOCIAL FATE happens to all of us at one time or another in our lives! Making mistakes and upsetting others, at times, is just what is called "being human." We know that people don't want to upset others most of the time, but it happens! When it does happen, use your problem solving skills.

This means you should think back to the choice you made that put you on the road to SOCIAL FATE. If a similar situation comes up again in the future, make the choice that will mostly likely put you on the road to SOCIAL FORTUNE. Why? Because this is the road that not only helps others to feel pretty good about you, but also helps you to feel good about yourself!

Remember, it is not a problem to make a mistake! It's only a problem when you don't learn from your mistakes!

FINAL TIP: If you landed on the road to SOCIAL FATE by accident – don't sweat it (meaning don't panic). One way to get back on the right road is to apologize to the person who might have been offended or hurt. Apologies are a way of letting others know that, although you made a mistake, you were thinking about them in a good way.

MEET THE CHARACTERS

JT

Rin

SOCIAL FORTUNE

OR

SOCIAL FATE

A SOCIAL THINKING® GRAPHIC NOVEL MAP FOR SOCIAL QUEST SEEKERS

WATCH THEIR DESTINIES UNFOLD BASED ON THE CHOICES THEY MAKE

Social FATE–Been There, Know That

SOCIAL SITUATION: Participating in a class discussion

Unexpected Behaviors... What you DO in the social situation	How others FEEL about what you did	How others treat you based on their feelings	How you FEEL about how they treated you
• Blurt the answer when it comes into your head • Show everyone that you know more than they do	• Frustrated • Annoyed	• Nag you • Ignore you • May not want to work with you • May talk about you behind your back	• Angry • Frustrated • Annoyed

QUEST TIP:
YOU KNOW IT, WE KNOW IT, DON'T BLOW IT!

You know it, but don't blow it by acting like a "know it all." The hidden rule, when you've got a head full of facts, is that you tell your information in small pieces. If you take over the class talking time with your knowledge, no one else gets a chance to be a part of the discussion. Others in the classroom will definitely have thoughts about this endless fact-spouting, and their thoughts won't be so good. Instead, be proud that you've got the wisdom and learn how to wield your smarts wisely. A *little can go a long way*, which means that talking about a little bit of what you know can help you be a better part of the classroom group. If you tell a lot of what you know, students may think you are trying to show them that you are smarter than they are. Peers hate it when other peers intentionally act like they are the smartest.

WHAT HAPPENED?

In this case, Kiko knew he was the expert on this topic and made the choice to let everyone in the room know about it. So what's the problem with that? After all, he was just saying the facts, right? Well...it doesn't work that way. Because he suggested to his classmates that he knew more than them, they thought of him as a "show-off" and became frustrated and maybe even embarrassed by the way he talked to them. His teacher was annoyed that he didn't follow the obvious (or hidden) rule that he needed to limit how much he shared to avoid accidentally putting down other students. In the end, Kiko ended up feeling upset and angry about how he was treated. If you look at the last box, you can see that he didn't realize that his choice was actually the catalyst (a thing that makes other things happen) that caused negative thoughts and emotions in everyone...including himself!

Have you ever been in this situation or seen something like this happen in a class?

OPTION: If you haven't already read about Kiko's success on the SOCIAL FORTUNE road, you could flip the book and do it now.

SOCIAL FATE–Speak Nothin' but the Truth

SOCIAL SITUATION: Someone you like (or are friends with) does something different with their appearance

Unexpected Behaviors... What you DO in the social situation	How others FEEL about what you did	How others treat you based on their feelings	How you FEEL about how they treated you
• Tell them you think it looks awful • Make a disgusted face	• Angry • Hurt	• May want to get away from you • Avoid you next time • May have an unhappy look on their face • May sound frustrated	• Hurt • Confused

The hidden rule is that we don't always say what pops into our heads. It's OK to think whatever you want, but when it comes to putting it into words—use caution. You have to think about how your words will impact the feelings of others because as the map above shows, eventually it comes back around to your own feelings. So the tip is to "filter" your thoughts before they come out of your mouth. Some things stay in your head (inside the filter), and some things can slip through the filter once you decide that what you have to say won't upset others. This is especially important when you want people to have reasonably good thoughts about you!

QUEST TIP: FILTER, FILTER, FILTER!

WHAT HAPPENED?

In this case, JT was surprised by Rin's new hair and his face showed it. The first thing that popped into his head was, "It looks awful; what were you thinking?" JT had always been taught that he needs to be honest and in fact, this has always been one of JT's greatest strengths...his honesty. So here's the scoop on this. One of the hidden rules of interacting with friends is that we have to be very careful when it comes to commenting—especially when it's about a person's appearance or intelligence. You might argue, "Well, she asked what he thought so he needed to tell her." Nope—we're here to tell you that this is the ultimate test of our BRAIN FILTER. By the time we're in middle school and high school, we need to actively use the filter every day. In other words, think whatever you want, but remember to think about how what you say or do will affect another's thoughts and feelings about you. After all, people treat you a certain way based on how they feel. And as you can see by JT's confused response in the end...sometimes it's just not worth it. JT needed to use the **Social Fake** to act like he thought it was OK even if he didn't like it at all if he wanted Rin to continue to think of him as friendly. Remember, in the long run, it's more important JT has people to talk to and who support him, rather than for him to always tell the absolute truth, when the truth hurts other's feelings.

What do you think? Was JT an Auto-Pilot Reactor or Option Resistor? What other options did he have in this situation?

OPTION: There was another way to handle this situation. If you haven't already done it, flip the novel over and see what happens when JT makes a different choice OR just keep reading to see what happens.

SOCIAL FATE–Bored Outta My Brain

SOCIAL SITUATION: Being a part of the learning group during a boring moment

Unexpected Behaviors... What you DO in the social situation	How others FEEL about what you did	How others treat you based on their feelings	How you FEEL about how they treated you
• Put your head down on the desk • Announce your boredom	• Angry • Frustrated • Irritated	• Consequences at school • Kids nag you • May get lunch detention • Teacher repeats lesson tomorrow	• Furious • Embarrassed

QUEST TIP: BOREDOM IS JUST A PART OF BEING HUMAN – DEAL WITH IT!

So here's the truth about life and school and people…they can be boring sometimes. We all have to learn to deal with the boring moments across the day. Everybody has to do it! How you deal with those moments eventually affects how others feel about you, how they treat you, and eventually how you feel about yourself. When you were really little, it was OK to announce to your parents that you were bored. In school, however, the hidden rule is that we just cope with the boring moment. It's what we do if we're bored while we're having a conversation with someone or when we are just sitting around others even if we are not talking to them. We've got a pretty cool strategy that is helpful for these boring times called the Social Fake. The SOCIAL FORTUNE map for this social situation has more info about this. The Social Fake is something everyone does once in awhile. It basically means that when something is boring, you don't announce it but instead keep your eyes and body focused on the other person while your brain takes a super-quick break. In other words, your thoughts might wander for a second or two when something is boring, but then (after your brain has a quick stretch) you tune into the person or situation again.

WHAT HAPPENED?

So in this situation, you can see that everyone is bored at some point during the teacher's discussion. Some students yawn, some stretch, and some do the Social Fake. In this case, Kiko became bored, like a lot of kids, and made the choice (Auto-Pilot Reactor or Option Resister?) to not only put his head on his desk to show his boredom…but announce it to the class as well. Bad idea. This not only irritated the teacher but the other students as well because they were all enduring the boring moment quietly. The big problem happened when there were consequences for Kiko and his classmates because the teacher decided to continue the lesson to the next day based on Kiko's behavior. As you can see, Kiko's choice made him feel furious AND he felt like the teacher had picked on him. He didn't see the connection between his choice, how it made others feel and how he felt in the end. Kiko could have used a Social Fortune Behavior Map early on to help him make a better choice and avoid the chain of events that happened.

How about you? What do you do when you're bored? Do you announce it to the class and teacher? If so, you're heading down this road of SOCIAL FATE! What are some better options for you? What road would you take in this situation?

Social FATE–It's Doomsday! (Or Is It?)

SOCIAL SITUATION: Time to finish homework

Unexpected Behaviors...What you DO in the social situation	How others FEEL about what you did	How others treat you based on their feelings	How you FEEL about how they treated you
• Big reaction to little problem • Throw your papers on the floor and refuse to work • Scream at others/complain	• Frustrated • Irritated	• May lose privileges (e.g., can't go online) • Nag you • Mom may yell back	• Awful • Mad • Stressed

Problems come in all sizes and range from nice and cool (size 1-3: little problem) to frustrating/irritating (size 4-7): moderate problem to red hot, boiling (size 8-10: big problem). Sometimes in the moment, each problem seems like it's a blazing 10, but it's really not. The first trick is to put your problem in perspective and figure out the actual size of the problem. You can do this by trying to think about how big others might see the problem. The second part is to realize that how you react to your perceived problem should be calmer than how the problem actually feels inside of you. This is especially true for small or moderate size problems. Take a few minutes to fill out the Size of the Problem Thermometer in the middle of this book. Think about a huge disaster (like an earthquake or a tornado or a car crash) and make that a size 10 problem. Your reaction really would and should be a 10 reaction (scream and cry and stuff). So if something that gigantic is a size 10, losing your game controller or finishing up the last four math problems is more like a size 3 problem—at most! And size 3 problems should have a minimal reaction like this—"Ugghhh"—and that's it! See more about this concept of size of the problem and compressing the size of your emotional response in the lessons reviewed at the start of this book.

QUEST TIP: TAKE YOUR PROBLEM'S TEMPERATURE!

WHAT HAPPENED?

So Rin always thinks that homework time is the end of the world. Whenever it's time to get going, she starts to "ramp up" her emotions (meaning she begins talking about and then increasing her anger and worry), feeling that she won't finish in time to do something else she wants to do. In this case, she had a BIG reaction by throwing her papers on the floor and yelling at her mom. Once she reacted with such strong negative emotions, this created a problem for her mother who now perceived Rin's real problem to be her inability to stay calm. Her mom was frustrated by Rin's inability to use emotional self-control and so her mom reacted with her own stronger emotional response. Her mom wasn't even concerned about Rin's math problems, she was more concerned about how upset Rin became! Rin forgot to stop and ask herself how BIG the problem really was and to use self-calming strategies to keep herself and others around her calm. We know that it's hard for some kids to figure out the size of a problem because all problems seem like they're really huge. We're here to tell you that problems really do come in different sizes, and you'll be able to figure this out with practice which includes discussion with others. It helps to get others' opinions about different kinds of problems and how they would rank the problem (tiny, so-so, huge). As you can see by what happened to Rin, her reaction caused her mom to think, "That was an overreaction" and her mom felt frustrated and irritated. So... what happens when mom gets frustrated about homework? Yep, you guessed it...now her mom has a reason to nag Rin about finishing the homework and Rin ended up with a punishment as well. Yikes...Rin ended up feeling awful and her mom was worried that Rin was not learning how to manage her emotions.

OPTION: Flip the book back over and compare the last box of the story. You can see how differently Rin feels in the end! Take a few minutes to think about what kinds of things seem like a size 10 (really big), size 5 (medium) or size 1-2 (small) problem for you. Are you an Option-Resister, Auto-Pilot Reactor, or Social Thinker when problems come your way?

SOCIAL FATE–I Don't Have a Clue

SOCIAL SITUATION: Figuring out what to say to others

Unexpected Behaviors... What you DO in the social situation	How others FEEL about what you did	How others treat you based on their feelings	How you FEEL about how they treated you
• Look away from group or look at the ground • Move body away from the group • Avoid making any comments or asking questions • Avoid hanging out around others	• Uncomfortable • Confused	• May walk away from you • May avoid you next time	• Angry • Frustrated

QUEST TIP: THINK, MOVE, LISTEN, AND GUESS!

Sometimes you might think it's easier to avoid people than try to figure out what to say to them. You might even think that if you just stand or sit far away from others and keep your eyes on the ground, no one will notice. We're here to tell you that people DO notice and have thoughts and feelings because of it. They notice when someone walks away from the group or always sits by himself or avoids being around the group. They may try to figure out why he is acting this way and then think: Is he unfriendly? Is he mad at them? Does he think he's better than them? So, use your social investigative tools to think about others, move to get into the group, listen to what they're talking about, and then make a Smart Guess (more on this Strategy Code on the road to SOCIAL FORTUNE).

WHAT HAPPENED?

JT is a guy who really wants to be a part of the group. He's nice and has a lot to contribute, but in this case, he chose to avoid the group rather than use a strategy. Here's the bummer—he already knew Kiko so he'd conquered the challenge of knowing another person in the group. Because of that, he was able to get his body in the group and greet Kiko. But then, his brain wasn't very flexible. He figured that because he didn't have that exact teacher, he couldn't connect with the guys. If he had used the Smart Guess strategy, he could have connected. Instead, he moved away from the group and stood by himself. He figured if he didn't talk, no one would notice him standing by himself. Well, that isn't the case because people do notice and they have thoughts about WHY you moved away from them or are standing alone. In this example, the other guys ended up feeling uncomfortable because they couldn't figure out JT's reason (or motive) for moving away. That made everyone simply walk away, and JT was confused and angry because of it. He didn't see that his choice made others have thoughts, feelings, and reactions. In the long run, JT felt left out and his peers felt it was too hard to try and figure out how to interact with JT.

OPTION: There was another way that JT could have handled this situation. Flip the book over and read about what happens when he makes a Smart Guess.

SOCIAL FATE–Huh?

SOCIAL SITUATION: Getting help in the classroom

Unexpected Behaviors... What you DO in the social situation	How others FEEL about what you did	How others treat you based on their feelings	How you FEEL about how they treated you
• Get mad about the work and give up • Blurt out: "This is stupid!" • Destroy paper and pencil • Avoid asking for help	• Annoyed • Frustrated • Impatient	• Might nag you • You may lose privileges • May avoid working with you • May ask you to leave the group or room	• Furious • Embarrassed

None of us were born wired to the Internet or pre-loaded with ALL knowledge, so it's a pretty good bet that we don't know every fact out there. That means that we ALL have to ask for help sometime. But, it's not just about asking. First you have to know when you need it. Once you know you need help, it's only a matter of asking. Well, HOW you ask can be an issue too, but that's covered on the map above and its related map on the SOCIAL FORTUNE side of this book. One strategy for knowing you need help is to be aware of when you're getting frustrated when you're learning something new or trying something different. If you're getting frustrated, you probably need some help. Then, when you feel that way, think, "Do I know what to do here?" If not—ask for help by raising your hand, staying calm, looking at the teacher, and then waiting for the teacher to call on you or come over to give you help. There are times you can also ask a peer for help and there may be times your peers ask you for help as well!

QUEST TIP: YOU CAN'T KNOW EVERYTHING!

WHAT HAPPENED?

Well, Kiko started out OK in this social situation. He didn't know what to do—which happens to everyone at some time or another—and so he looked around the room. He saw that other kids were struggling too, but this is where he turned down the road to SOCIAL FATE. His inner coach and filter strategies (see the Social Fortune road for more about this) were nowhere to be found, so Kiko reacted by yelling out, "This is stupid!" By doing this, Kiko made his teacher frustrated that he was having an outburst again in class, and the other kids in the class were just plain annoyed. The class had to stop for a few minutes while the teacher sent Kiko out of the class. Now everyone, including Kiko, feels bad about the situation. In the end, Kiko became furious and started to really hate coming to that class. It could have been a completely different situation if Kiko had been a SOCIAL THINKER and used his strategy codes rather than becoming an Auto-Pilot Reactor!

OPTION: If you haven't already looked at the SOCIAL FORTUNE map, you might want to flip the book and check it out. This story has a better ending!

Social FATE—You Talkin' to Me?

SOCIAL SITUATION—Classroom lesson when you know the answer

Unexpected Behaviors... What you DO in the social situation	How others FEEL about what you did	How others treat you based on their feelings	How you FEEL about how they treated you
• Blurt out the answer	• Annoyed • Frustrated	• Teacher or peers may respond with angry words • May not want to work in your group	• Angry • Upset

QUEST TIP: AVOID THE BLURT!

We understand that it's a little frustrating when you know the right answer to a question in class and want to shout it out. The problem is that if you always say the answer when it's not your turn, you'll really annoy your teacher and other kids in the class. The trick is to figure out if it's your time to shine. Rin spaced out for a bit and then didn't use her eyes to figure out who the teacher was asking. So then Rin blurted out her answer and ended up annoying everyone around her. Your job is to "avoid the blurt," which means use your brain to think about focusing and your eyes to help you know when it's up to you to share your wisdom!!

WHAT HAPPENED?

Rin did what so many of us do when we're sitting in a group. Even though she really tried to focus on what the teacher was saying, she looked away for only a few seconds and her mind wandered (meaning she started thinking about other things). Suddenly, she re-focused and heard the teacher ask a question. She knew the answer (like Rin usually does) and blurted it out. This left the teacher frustrated and annoyed because he'd already talked to Rin about her blurting in class. The other kids in the class felt like Rin was showing off again and being a "know-it-all." So what happened next is what often happens—the teacher scolded Rin, and Rin's classmate not only told her to stop but also avoided her during the next group task. This left Rin feeling pretty lousy and angry.

Is blurting a difficult thing for you to control? It is for many kids, but it's something that you can get better at with practice. Take a closer look at the Strategy Codes Rin used on the road to SOCIAL FORTUNE and try using them in your own life.

OPTION: Keep reading about Rin, Kiko, and JT on this road to SOCIAL FATE or flip the book and see how they can change how they feel in the end because of the choice they make.

Social FATE— My Way or the Highway!

SOCIAL SITUATION – Working in a small group

Unexpected Behaviors... What you DO in the social situation	How others FEEL about what you did	How others treat you based on their feelings	How you FEEL about how they treated you
• Refuse to try things another way—rigid thinking • Tell kids their ideas are wrong or yell at them • Leave the group	• Irritated • Angry • Annoyed	• May avoid working with you in the future • Teacher and students have irritated looks on their faces • People have frustrated sounding voices	• Awful • Sad • Angry • Stressed

Seems pretty obvious that when you *think* you know the best way to do something that everyone else will just do it **your way**. Well, that's easier said than done when you work in a group. Everyone has opinions and ideas about how to do things. Most of the time the group needs flexible thinkers to simply get the project done. Flexible thinking is really at the core of being a *social thinker*. It's what allows us to consider another kid's ideas or let us play a game a different way or helps us to figure out another way to solve everyday problems. When JT was younger, he liked things to happen in a certain way and that was kinda OK. Now that he's older, the challenge for him is that it can't always be about what he wants. In fact, as we all get older, the lesson is—another way is still OK!

QUEST TIP: ANOTHER WAY IS STILL OK.

WHAT HAPPENED?

In this case, JT was sure that he knew exactly how to do the project in the most efficient way. The others in the group were showing some flexibility, but JT decided it was a HUGE problem and stormed away from the group. The other kids in his group ended up being really irritated and angry because the project came to a standstill (meaning it stopped) because of JT's inflexibility. He hoped that if he stormed away from the group and stood by himself, the teacher would let him work alone and then he could do it his own way. That didn't happen, and she sent him back to the group. Now the group members are feeling like JT is acting a little young for his age and delaying them from finishing the project. Too bad JT chose to be an Option Resister because he's the one who ended up feeling awful in the end.

Are you kinda rigid when it comes to doing something that's not exactly your way? Work on keeping your brain and thinking flexible and you'll avoid the road of SOCIAL FATE. What are some other options JT could have tried rather than leaving the group?

OPTION: Take a look at how JT figured this out by flipping the book to the SOCIAL FORTUNE road for this situation.

Social FATE–Who Changed the Rules?

SOCIAL SITUATION – Break time

Unexpected Behaviors... What you DO in the social situation	How others FEEL about what you did	How others treat you based on their feelings	How you FEEL about how they treated you
• Do what you want even if it's unexpected for the situation • Go play by yourself • Avoid the group	• Embarrassed • Mean	• May say mean things to you • May avoid you	• Embarrassed • Angry

Lots of kids your age are looking to find something "different" about others to then give them a hard time or tease them. In an ideal world, teasing would never happen. But we're not there yet. We think it's cool to be different or unique, and it's really OK to enjoy your own interests in a place where you know the people are SAFE (like home). But, when it comes to school…some kids simply look for an opportunity to be mean. Lots of kids still like to play with toys like they did when they were younger. In fact, we know of some adults who continue to like watching kid's cartoons or do other "kid-like" activities. The secret here is not to give up doing some of the things you've always loved but instead remember that the social rules change with age. If your peers see you acting at school in a manner they consider to be immature but observe you being pretty smart in other areas, they often think this is a reason to pick on you. The good news is that there are some strategy codes to help! Take a quick peek at the offensive strategies like FOR and RCA on the inside cover of the book and think about how the situation might have turned out differently. We are sorry to say, bullies continue to exist, but they'll have one less thing to bug you about.

QUEST TIP: STAY ALERT! THE RULES KEEP CHANGING!

WHAT HAPPENED?

In this case, Kiko knew the rules had changed because he's older, but he decided to do his own thing anyway. This is a classic example of an Option Resister. He thought about the consequences of his choice and decided to play anyway. Even though he had fun with this toys for a few minutes, it didn't last long. It would have been really easy for him to wait until he was at home and in his room before pulling them out. His actions made his friend Rin think, "Couldn't he wait until he goes home?" and she felt embarrassed for Kiko and herself. Rin knew that when Kiko took out his toys, others would think he was really immature. Being considered immature means others think that the person is following social rules of a younger age group. The reason this is a problem is that it is expected that all kids continue to keep acting older (more mature) with each passing month or year. Too bad Kiko didn't wait because there's always someone ready to make a rude comment about others, especially when the kid violates the Rules Change with Age law. It's a bummer because the person who ended up feeling angry and embarrassed was Kiko.

Are you someone who has interests that are a little younger than your peers at school? It's OK to have those interests, just know that the rules change with age and that you do have control over your choices. And remember, your choices affect the way you feel in the end.

OPTION: Flip the book to continue…or don't. But, while you're deciding take a minute to think about what some of the social rules are for you now and what they used to be when you were younger. Ask your teacher/parent or someone older to tell you about how the social rules have changed for them as they got older. Change is just one of those things that happens for everyone, so just keep working to figure them out!

Social FATE–Know When To Take A Detour
SOCIAL SITUATION – Sharing ideas/opinions

Unexpected Behaviors... What you DO in the social situation	How others FEEL about what you did	How others treat you based on their feelings	How you FEEL about how they treated you
• Tell peers what *to do* based on your opinions or knowledge • Tell peers what they shouldn't do • Forget to think about how people are thinking about you	• Annoyed • Angry	• May say rude things to you • May avoid you next time • May tell others about your comments to them	• Angry • Frustrated • Embarrassed

QUEST TIP:
WHEN IN DOUBT, TAKE ANOTHER ROUTE.

No doubt, many of us think we know a lot about something, and in fact you might be someone who knows a ton! That's not the point when it comes to being around your peers. Telling your opinion or stating the facts during social times is just plain annoying to most teens. This doesn't mean that you can't have opinions on things; you need to know WHEN to share them. Teens don't really like other teens to tell them what they can and can't do. You'd probably agree with this because we're pretty sure you don't like it when other kids tell you what you can and can't do! It can be annoying. But, here's the real issue: when others are upset or offended by you, they are more likely to treat you poorly. Avoid this by doing your best to think about how others are interpreting what you're saying to them or how they think you are treating them.

WHAT HAPPENED?

In JT's case, he decided he had a point to make but didn't think about the fact that he sounded like he was bossing his peers around. Both kids became very annoyed and started saying rude things—and not only did they say things about JT's chicken comments but began to tease him as well. The problem is that once an exchange like this happens, other kids remember. Sometimes kids will bring it up over and over hoping to get a reaction from you. It would have been a whole lot easier if JT had kept his thoughts in his head. On the other hand, if his peers had asked about what JT thought about eggs/chickens, it would have been OK to share his opinion. It's kinda tricky but as you can see by the map above…in the end, JT was really the only person who felt angry and embarrassed about the situation.

If you are someone who feels the need to get your point across to others because you think you're right…stop for a minute and think about what they are thinking about you! If you insist you are right you may well be frustrating or offending another person(s) which may make them want to treat you poorly in the future. Unfortunately, once a person upsets another person, the person who is upset may go complain to their friends. Now the upset peer has a team of people working against the instigator by treating him or her very poorly.

OPTION: If you started on the SOCIAL FATE side, you're finished with the graphic stories and the maps that go with them. It's time to flip the book to the other side and read the maps, Strategy Codes, and Quest Tips that made our characters follow the SOCIAL FORTUNE road.

Social FORTUNE

SOCIAL SITUATION

Important: The behaviors listed below aren't in any particular order. For example, the first behavior in column one doesn't have to match the first feeling in column two and so on.

Expected Behaviors... What you DO in the social situation	How others FEEL about what you did	How others treat you based on their feelings	How you FEEL about how they treated you
•	•	•	•

Fortune/23

Fate/22

How you FEEL about how they treated you	How others treat you based on their feelings	How others FEEL about what you did	Unexpected Behaviors... What you DO in the social situation
•	•	•	•

Important: The behaviors listed below aren't in any particular order. For example, the first behavior in column one doesn't have to match the first feeling in column two and so on.

SOCIAL SITUATION

Social FATE